My Best Book of

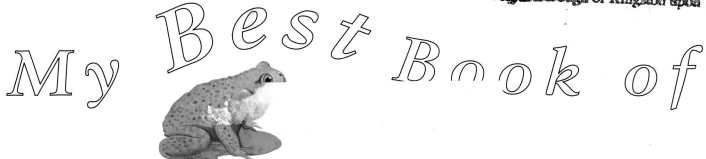

Night-time Animals

Belinda Weber

Contents

KINGFISHER

Kingfisher Publications Plc
New Penderel House
283–288 High Holborn
London WC1V 7HZ

www.kingfisherpub.com

Consultant: David Burnie
Managing editor: Carron Brown
Art director: Mike Davis
Assistant designer: Jack Clucas
DTP co-ordinator: Catherine Hibbert
Production controller: Jessamy Oldfield

Illustrations by Mark Bergin

First published by Kingfisher
Publications Plc 2006

10 9 8 7 6 5 4 3 2 1

1TR/0206/WKT/SCHOY/128KMA/C

ISBN-13: 978 0 7534 1301 2
ISBN-10: 0 7534 1301 9

Printed in China

Why are some animals active at night?

At night, when it is dark, most animals head for the safety of their homes, or find a quiet spot to sleep in. But others, called nocturnal animals, wake up and become active. They may need the cooler temperature that night brings to survive. Or they may prefer to lurk in the shadows, safe from predators.

Hunter and hunted

Cats are hunters that eat mice. They listen for tiny sounds that tell them where to find their prey. Mice also have good hearing. They listen for sounds of hunters.

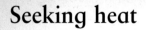

Seeking heat

Pit vipers do not need to see their prey. They have special holes, called pits, on their lips that detect heat. The snake can track an animal by its body heat.

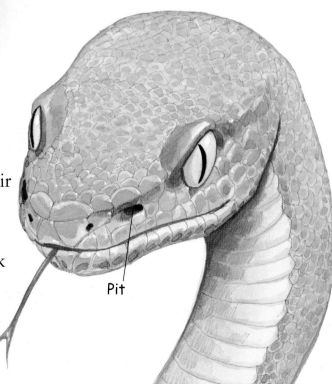

Pit

4

Life in the dark

Nocturnal animals often have larger eyes and ears to help them find their way in the dark. Frogs and toads need to keep cool to stop their skin from drying out. They keep out of the sunshine during the day and become more active at night.

Tree frogs can dry out in the fierce sun, so they are active at night

Fennec foxes have large ears and can hear very well

Tarsiers have big eyes which help them see well in the dark

5

The jungle at night

Even in the jungle of South America, lots of animals wake up when night falls. When howler monkeys call to each other, their voices can be heard up to five kilometres away. They are especially noisy at dusk and dawn, when their loud, roaring sounds let one another know where they are.

The owl monkey, or douroucouli, leaps between trees, looking for insects and fruit to eat ——

Three-toed sloth

Working shifts

By coming out at night, nocturnal animals avoid all the creatures that are active during the day. This means that they will not eat each other, or be competing with one another to eat the same food. By avoiding each other, all the animals can feed from the same trees.

Olingo

Owl monkey

Silky anteater

Desert life

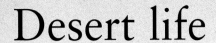

The North American desert is extremely hot during the day, so most of the animals come out at night. They spend their days in cool burrows or dens, or asleep in shady spots. The skin covering their ears is thin so the blood vessels are close to the surface. This helps the creatures keep cool.

Stink bombs

Skunks have an unusual way of defending themselves from attack. They squirt a jet of smelly liquid from under their tails. This makes it hard for the attacker to breathe, and the skunk can get away.

Little owl

Deer

Skunk

Scorpion

Cricket

8

Nighthawk

Little owl

Coyote

Kangaroo rat

Kit fox

9

Wild dogs

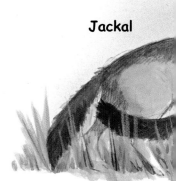

Wolves, jackals and dingos are all wild dogs. They have excellent vision and a good sense of smell. These senses help them track down their prey and also to stay together as a pack. Wolves are well known for their eerie howling at the moon. This tells the others in their group where they are and helps them stay in touch. They also use their tails and faces to communicate with each other and hunt together as a pack.

Jackal

Wolf

Hyena

Sharing food

Jackals and hyenas are scavengers as well as hunters. They hunt for themselves, and will also follow lions to steal their prey, or finish their leftovers. Hyenas have a dog-like shape, but they are not wild dogs.

Howling dogs

Dingos howl like wolves to keep in touch with each other. They hunt small mammals on their own, but will join up with other dingos to hunt larger prey.

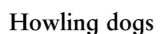

Strong hunters

Wolves are built to hunt. Their long, strong legs help them to run huge distances. Wolves have big stomachs, so can eat a lot at one time. They gorge themselves after a successful hunt, eating as much as nine kilograms of meat in one meal.

Dingo

11

Woodlands at night

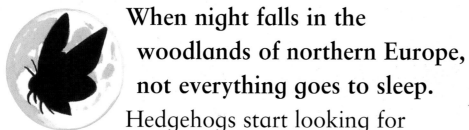

When night falls in the woodlands of northern Europe, not everything goes to sleep. Hedgehogs start looking for food. Foxes are clever hunters. They listen for prey and then sneak up on it. They can move their ears in the direction of a sound, and can even hear small animals digging under the ground.

Twilight zone

Deer settle in clearin[g] for the night. They [are] shy creatures and ar[e] most active during the late evenings and early mornings.

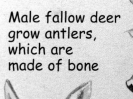

Male fallow deer grow antlers, which are made of bone

Eating worms

Badgers spend their days asleep in a burrow called a sett. They rummage

Hiding by day

Moths fly at night to avoid birds that might eat them. Their mottled colours help them blend in with bark or leaves while they rest during the day.

Moth

Tawny owl

Every evening, badgers leave their setts to look for food

Red fox

13

Night birds

Barn owl

Owls are hunters and catch their prey at night. They listen for the tiny squeaks and rustling sounds that small mammals make as they search for food in the undergrowth. Once they have found their prey, owls swoop through the air to catch it. They have sharp claws on their feet with which they grab their victims, and sharp beaks to tear up the flesh.

Long-eared owl

Silent hunters

Many owls have soft, fluffy fringes on their wing feathers. These help the owls to fly silently, and pounce on their victims without being heard. In the quiet, the owl can concentrate on listening for sounds of its animal food.

Big ears

Long-eared owls prefer to hunt over open countryside. Like most owls, they have one of their ear holes slightly higher than the other. This helps them work out exactly where a sound is coming from, so that they can home in on their prey. Long-eared owls spend their days resting in trees.

14

Slow flyer

Barn owls have flat, heart-shaped faces with big eyes. Their hearing is excellent and they use their ears to find rodent prey. Once they have found a victim, they fly slowly and quietly, close to the ground, until they catch it.

15

Moonlit seas

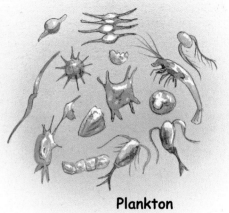

Even in the murky depths of the seas, day and night are important. Some fish spend their days in the calm, deep waters but rise to the surface to feed during the quiet of the night. Others swim near the surface during the day and return to the deeper water overnight. Going up or down, the fish must always swim past other fish that want to eat them.

Plankton

Herring

Swimming jellies

Common jellyfish follow small fish on their nightly journey to the surface. Any fish that brushes against a jellyfish's stinging tentacles is paralyzed and eaten.

Minute plankton

Millions of tiny animals, called plankton, rise through the water to feed at the surface each evening. Thousands of other fish follow the plankton up, to feast on them and each other.

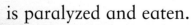

Toothy hunters

Whitetip reef sharks cruise the moonlit
waters looking for food. They sleep by day,
hiding in caves or lurking on the sea floor,
to avoid any predators that might eat them.

17

Wetlands

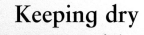

Rivers, swamps and wetlands provide homes for many nocturnal animals. Otters, alligators, frogs and toads hunt at night, making good use of the darkness to help them find their prey. The flowing water of a river offers a variety of places for animals to find food or shelter. However, animals have to be careful that they are not washed away.

Snappy hunter

American alligators are huge, growing up to 5.5 metres long. They are not fussy eaters, but will tuck in to anything they can catch, including turtles and birds.

Keeping dry

Otters eat fish and spend a lot of time in the river chasing them. Their fur is waterproof and their feet are webbed to help them swim. They are expert swimmers, and they use their flattened tails like a rudder to help them steer.

Saving some for later

Water voles make their nests beside
the river. They are good swimmers,
and eat water plants, roots, bulbs
and fallen fruit. They sometimes
store extra food in their nests.

American alligator

Noisy neighbours

When a bullfrog searches for a mate, the
male 'calls' loudly. It has a pouch under
its chin that blows up like a balloon.
This makes the sound much louder,
so it can be heard from further away.

19

Furry flyers

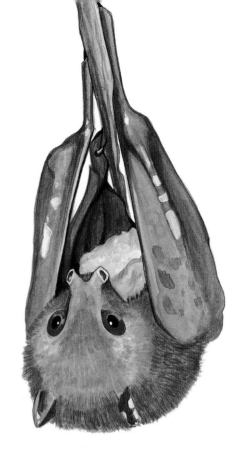

Bats are shy creatures that fly at night to avoid birds that might eat them. During the day, these animals stay hidden, roosting in caves, trees or under the roofs of buildings. Bats are the only mammals that can fly. Their wings are made of skin stretched between the bats' long fingers. Different types of bat eat different foods. Many feed on fruit and flowers, but others are hunters.

Messy eaters

Fruit bats squash fruit into their mouths, drinking the juice. They drop any seeds or pulp on the ground.

Listening for food

Some bats let out a high-pitched squeak. If this sound hits an insect, some of the sound bounces back. The echo lets the bat know where its food is. This is called echolocation.

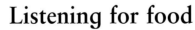

An echo of the bat's squeak lets it know where its insect prey is

Sounds like lunch

Long-eared bats hunt
night-flying insects. They
can turn their large ears in
many directions to pick up
even the smallest of sounds.

Blood for dinner

Vampire bats are shy and nervous. They
land near a cow and then scuttle closer,
crawling on their wings. They bite their
victims with sharp teeth, then lap up
the blood. Vampire bats prefer cows'
blood but will sometimes bite humans.

An African night

Darkness brings many predators on to the African plains. Baboons settle down to sleep in nests made high in the trees. Hippos leave the cool water of lakes where they wallow during the day to stop their skin burning in the sun's heat. At night, when it is cooler, they come out to graze on the lush grasses.

Safety in numbers

With leopards and lions hunting them, gazelles gather in large herds. Here many eyes and ears are listening for danger.

Gazelle

Hippo

Baboon

Mongooses have thick
fur to protect them
from snakes, which
they hunt for food

Leopard

Royal python

Mongoose

23

Cat empire

Many big cats sneak up on their prey while they are asleep at night. Like other big cats, tigers have soft, fleshy pads on their feet that help them to walk quietly, letting them creep up on their prey. Many cats' eyes have long, thin pupils that look like slits. In the dark, these slits widen to let in as much light as possible. This helps the cats see in the moonlight so they can hunt their prey.

Hunted
Ocelots'
beautifully
patterned fur
fetches high prices
in the fashion world.
So many of these cats
have been killed that this
trade has now been banned.

Water cats

South American jaguars like to eat
fish, which they scoop out of the
water with their large paws. Unlike
many cats, jaguars love water and
are very good swimmers.

25

Night in the bush

In the heat of the Australian bush, many animals prefer the cooler temperatures of the night. Echidnas snuffle about, searching for ants and termites, which they suck up with their long tongues. They are good diggers and can break open termites' nests with their strong claws. Kangaroos travel to new feeding grounds by night, covering longer distances than they could by day.

Kangaroo

Giant heads

Cassowaries are large birds that live in Australia's rainforests, and are active at dusk and dawn. They have large bony shields, called casques, on the tops of their heads. These protect their heads as they push their way through the plant life.

Possum

Sugar glider

Koala

Phalanger

Sleepy koala

Koalas eat eucalyptus leaves, which are hard to digest. The koala does not get much energy from its food so it sleeps a lot. It does not need to drink very often as it gets all the moisture it needs from its leafy food. Koala is an Aboriginal word that means 'no drink'.

Echidna

Bugs galore

Thousands of bugs wake up at night and search for food. They creep, scuttle and slither around, trying not to be seen by anything that might eat them. The only time they make themselves seen or heard is when they are looking for a mate. Crickets sing noisily to tell others where they are. Glow-worms flash pulses of light, signalling their position to others.

Hairy legs

Bird-eating spiders hunt at night. Hairs on their legs pick up vibrations in the air, alerting them to their prey moving close by.

Stinging tails

Scorpions are clever hunters that lurk by their lairs waiting for prey to creep by. They grab their victim with their pincer-like claws, or paralyze them with their poisonous stinging tails.

Creepy cockroach

Cockroaches are one of the fastest insects. When threatened, they dart into dark cracks to hide.

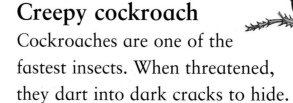

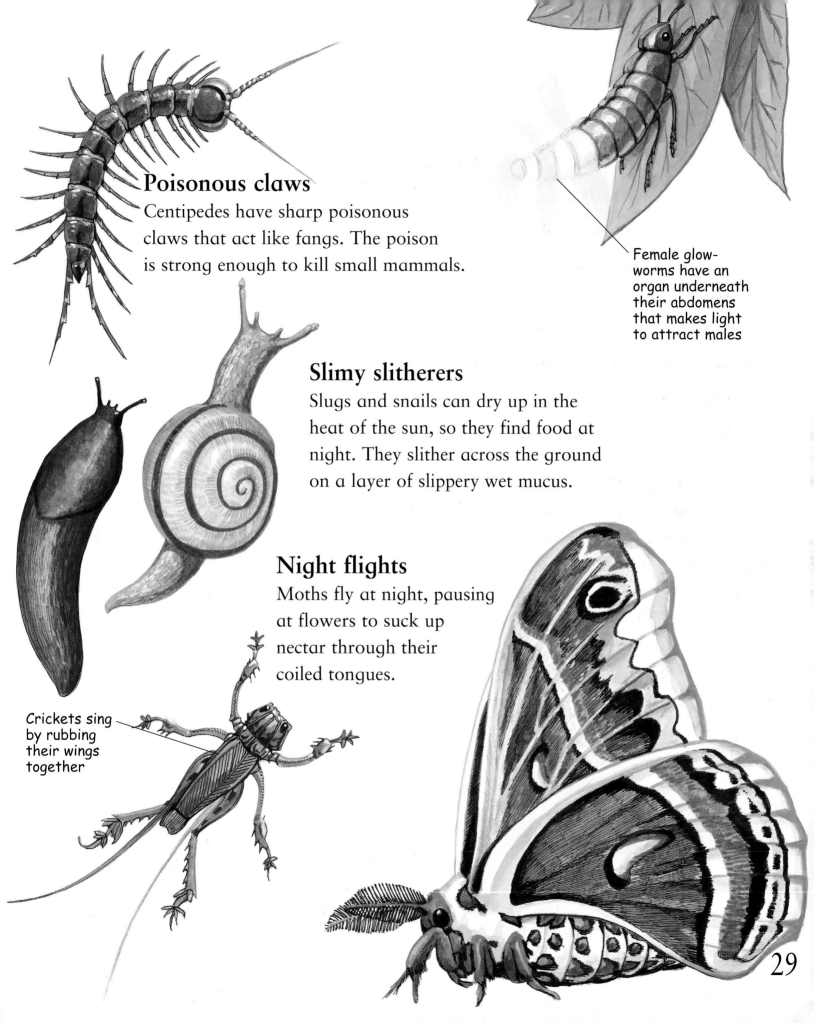

Poisonous claws

Centipedes have sharp poisonous claws that act like fangs. The poison is strong enough to kill small mammals.

Female glow-worms have an organ underneath their abdomens that makes light to attract males

Slimy slitherers

Slugs and snails can dry up in the heat of the sun, so they find food at night. They slither across the ground on a layer of slippery wet mucus.

Night flights

Moths fly at night, pausing at flowers to suck up nectar through their coiled tongues.

Crickets sing by rubbing their wings together

29

Raiders of the night

Animals need room to live, but people have to build houses to make homes for themselves. Many animals have learned to live among people. Gardens and parks have become their homes, and animals feed on the scraps of food left behind, as well as the plants that grow there. Rats and mice find plenty to eat from people's leftovers, and larger animals, such as foxes and raccoons, raid dustbins.

Hungry raccoons

Raccoons are woodland creatures, but they have learned to live with humans. They have a good sense of smell and are excellent at climbing. They can get into rubbish bins, and often feast on leftover food.

Raccoon

Glossary

abdomen The third, or rear, part of an insect's body.

Aboriginal Aborigines were the first people to live in Australia. Aboriginal describes something that has come from Aborigines.

bush Open scrubland in Australia.

communicate To pass messages between one another with sounds or body language.

competing Trying to outdo another to find food or a mate.

detect To find.

digest To absorb nutrients and energy from one's food.

mammal A warm-blooded animal that feeds its young on milk.

mottled Irregular patterns or markings on the skin that help break up an animal's shape.

mucus Slime produced by the body.

paralyzed Unable to move.

predator An animal that hunts and kills other animals for food.

prey Animals that are hunted and eaten by other animals.

pupils The black parts of eyes that open to let in light.

rodent A small mammal, such as a mouse or rat.

rudder A device used to help steer a boat.

scavenger An animal that eats food that is already dead.

tentacles Long, frilly strings or legs.

track To find and follow.

trade The buying and selling of goods, in this case animal skins.

undergrowth Small plants and leaf-litter that are found close to the ground.

vibrations Movements in the air that help a predator find its prey.

Index

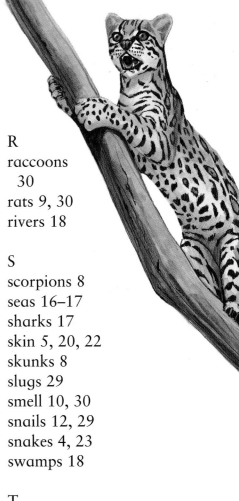

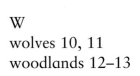